Hampton National Historic Site Guidebook

Hampton National
Historic Site Guidebook

The Donning Company Publishers
184 Business Park Drive, Suite 206
Virginia Beach, VA 23462

Library of Congress Cataloging-in-Publication Data

Hampton National Historic Site guidebook / by the staff of the Hampton
National Historic Site.
      p.   cm.
   ISBN 978-1-57864-631-9 (soft cover : alk. paper)
1. Hampton National Historic Site (Md.)—Guidebooks. 2. Historic buildings—
Maryland—Baltimore County—Guidebooks. 3. Mansions—Maryland—
Baltimore County—Guidebooks. 4. Towson (Md.)—Buildings, structures,
etc.—Guidebooks. 5. Towson (Md.)—History. 6. Towson (Md.)—Biography. 7.
Ridgely family. I. Hampton National Historic Site (Agency : U.S.)
   F187.B2H36 2010
   975.2'71—dc22

                                                  2010023401

Printed in the USA at Walsworth Publishing Company

On the back cover: Watercolor view of Hampton mansion by Robert Carey
Long, Jr., 1838; private collection.

Contents

Preface

Visiting Hampton National Historic Site

One visitor described Hampton as the "showplace" of America, stating that there "is nothing like it south of Mason and Dixon's line." The grand mansion, grounds, and surrounding outbuildings impressed visitors since the eighteenth century to the present day. For more than 150 years Hampton was the home of the Ridgely family. Originally built as a summer house, it served as the centerpiece of an agricultural and industrial complex that numbered over twenty-five thousand acres at its height in the early nineteenth century.

The seven generations of the Ridgely family left their legacy as seen through the collections, outbuildings, and changes to the landscape itself. Over 90 percent of the objects on view at Hampton are original to the estate, and each room of the Mansion is furnished to a different era of time. These, together with the Lower (Overseer's) House, Slave Quarters, Dairy, and Formal Gardens offer a rare and complete touchstone to America's past. Ranger-led tours of the Mansion tell the engaging story of entrepreneurs, indentured servants, slaves, and the changing face of America through the colorful history of the Ridgely family.

A site visit includes the farm side with historic Lower House, Slave Quarters, and Dairy

The grounds are open daily except for Thanksgiving, Christmas, and New Year's Day; hours vary seasonally. Please check the website for Mansion tours. Be advised that the Mansion and the outbuildings are closed on certain days during the winter months. Please check the website: www.nps.gov/hamp for current updates.

The website of Hampton's friend's group, Historic Hampton Inc., www.historichampton.org, provides additional information on the site and special events.

By Car: Hampton National Historic Site is close to three Interstate Highways—Routes 695, 70, and 95. From the Baltimore Beltway (I 695) eastbound or westbound: Take Exit 27B, Dulaney Valley Road northbound. Take the first right turn onto Hampton Lane. The park will be on your right, about one-half mile from the intersection.
Hampton National Historic Site
535 Hampton Lane
Towson, MD 21286

Public Transportation: Bus No. 11 stops at Goucher College, less than one mile from Hampton. The Light Rail stop at Lutherville is approximately three miles from Hampton. From either stop, we recommend that you do not walk to the park because there are no sidewalks. We suggest that you use a taxi.

Want to follow your GPS receiver to our front door? Enter one of these sets of numbers: Latitude/Longitude: N 39 degrees 24.987 minutes W 076 degrees 35.267 minutes.

Carriage rides past the Mansion are a special program at Hampton NHS

Introduction

Hampton National Historic Site, once the center of a vast Maryland land holding and a premiere example of Georgian architecture and landscape design, was a remarkable commercial, industrial and agricultural estate forged with indentured and enslaved labor. Hampton reflects a central irony in American history: that a nation newly established on the principles of equality and freedom could accept the institution of slavery. The centerpiece of the park, which preserves the heart of the Ridgely family estate dating back to the 1700s, is the elegantly furnished Hampton Mansion. Set amid formal gardens and shade trees, it was one of the largest private residences in the United States when completed in 1790.

View from Hampton Mansion looking north to the Lower House (photo: Richard Anderson)

In 1745, the first Ridgely to make his mark on this place acquired a fifteen-hundred-acre tract which had all the essential elements for iron-making. By 1762, when Colonel Charles Ridgely established an ironworks, iron was one of the most profitable exports in the mid-Atlantic colonies. Buoyed by ownership in the ironworks, mills, quarries, orchards, and a general merchandising business in Baltimore, his son Charles amassed enough wealth to build an elegant country seat, as well as sow the seeds of his heirs' fortunes.

The Mansion reflects classic Georgian symmetry: a large three-story structure connected to smaller wings on either side by hyphens. The exterior is constructed of stone quarried on Ridgely property, stuccoed over and scored to resemble blocks of limestone. Although the Mansion did not have a formal architect, master builder Jehu Howell is credited with much of the design. Local craftsmen, the enslaved and indentured servants provided the labor.

The Ridgelys lived in a manner befitting their stature as illustrated by this elegant country seat. They hosted lavish parties, bred and raced Thoroughbred horses, imported Madeira, and consolidated their power through public office. The Ridgelys indulged their taste for fine furnishings. The set of Baltimore-made painted furniture in the drawing room reflects a passion for the styles of ancient Greece and Rome. Other Ridgely generations updated the furnishings to high Victorian taste, resulting in today's significant museum collection of decorative arts.

Aerial photo of Hampton NHS and the surrounding neighborhood, 1953

A large cadre of workers supported this way of life. Hampton's labor force included free artisans and tradesmen, indentured servants, and convict laborers. By far the most important component of the work force, however, was slaves. The enslaved worked in every capacity. Hampton's slave population at its height numbered more than three hundred, making it one of the largest slaveholding plantations in Maryland. Extant buildings include two Slave Quarters, a rarity in historic structures. The archival collections also include extensive primary source material about Hampton's enslaved. Slave inventories, Ridgely family diaries, memoirs, and business accounts provide a picture of African-American life on the estate.

In the late eighteenth century, formal geometric gardens set on terraced earthworks were created on the south side of the Mansion, while on the north side stretched a landscaped park. In the 1830s and 1840s, Ridgely family members enhanced the "natural" landscape with exotic plantings, several of which have grown into Maryland State Champion Trees. Today the formal gardens are restored to their original nineteenth-century appearance.

At the height of their fortunes, the Ridgely's property equaled half the area of present-day Baltimore city. Today's 63-acre park, which preserves the Mansion and its immediate surroundings, is a remnant of the Hampton estate of the early 1800s. It was owned by descendents of the Ridgely family until 1948 when, based on outstanding architectural merit, the Mansion and the core of the Hampton property were designated a National Historic Site. In 1978, the 14.02-acre farm site was added to the park, ensuring the stories of the working estate were represented. The site was managed by the Society for the Preservation of Maryland Antiquities, until the National Park Service took over operations in 1979.

Come and explore Hampton National Historic Site. United States history is brought to life through seven generations of one elite family and the slaves, indentured servants, and paid workers who supported them—spanning the period from before the American Revolution to after World War II. Hampton is a microcosm of life in the mid-Atlantic region, reflecting two hundred years of American social, historical, and economic development. Individually, many of Hampton National Historic Site's cultural and natural resources are important; taken together, its numerous assets and the extensive related documentation make it a resource of great significance to its local community, the state of Maryland, and the nation.

1

Hampton
1745–1783

T he estate known as Hampton evolved from various tracts of land acquired by the Ridgely family starting with the 1500-acre "Northampton" tract in 1745. Other portions included "Oakhampton" and "Hampton Court." The name "Hampton" likely originated with Colonel Henry Darnall, a relative of Lord Baltimore for whom the property had originally been surveyed in 1695. Darnall bequeathed Northampton to his daughter, Ann Hill (1680–1749). She and her sons, Henry and Clement, sold the tract to Colonel Charles Ridgely in 1745 for 600 pounds sterling.

Portrait of Captain Charles Ridgely the Builder by John Hesselius, ca. 1765

The "Northampton" tract came to Colonel Ridgely with houses, outhouses, tobacco houses, barns, stables, gardens, and orchards. By 1750, Colonel Ridgely owned more than eight thousand acres of land in Baltimore and Anne Arundel Counties. In addition to his interests as a plantation owner and planter, he was a successful merchant and served in the Maryland Legislature as a representative for Baltimore County.

Recognizing the greater economic opportunity of ironmaking over tobacco farming, Colonel Ridgely

Portrait of Rebecca Dorsey Ridgely by John Hesselius, ca. 1765

established an ironworks in partnership with his sons, John and Charles. Probably not coincidentally, his younger son Captain Charles (so called because he was a mariner and ship's captain) married Rebecca Dorsey (1739–1812), the daughter of Caleb Dorsey, a prominent and wealthy Anne Arundel County ironmaster. Northampton Furnace and Forges, formally established in 1762 and the tenth ironworks in Maryland, took advantage of the easily mined deposits of iron ore in the area. The Northampton Company was to make a substantial fortune for the Ridgelys both before and during the American Revolutionary War.

Captain Ridgely had served in the 1750s as a ship's captain for the mercantile firm James Russell and Company. His maritime adventures included quelling a mutiny, surviving two hurricanes, and being imprisoned by the French during the French and Indian War. In 1763, he retired from the sea and assumed control of the family iron business,

Telescope by Cox, London, originally owned by Captain Ridgely, ca. 1770

Iron fireback from the Northampton Ironworks, ca. 1770

while remaining an active agent for British merchants until the Revolutionary War. In addition to the mercantile business in Baltimore Town, Captain Ridgely owned vast farms cultivating grain and vegetable crops; bred cattle, pigs, and Thoroughbred horses; planted commercial orchards; and operated mills and quarries. An active politician and member of the Maryland Legislature, he was the acknowledged political boss of Baltimore County.

After the death of his brother John in 1771 and his father in 1772, Captain Charles Ridgely owned a two-thirds share in the Northampton Ironworks and maintained control of the entire operation. The Northampton Ironworks was a labor-intensive business which relied on a large and diverse workforce of slaves, indentured servants, convict laborers and—during the Revolutionary War—even British prisoners of war. The war created an ever-growing market for the forge's products such as shot, cannons, and camp kettles. Income from this enterprise permitted Captain Ridgely to acquire thousands of acres of land confiscated from the British immediately following the War, and he eventually owned more than twenty-four thousand acres.

Pewter soup plates made by John Townsend, London, with the initials of Captain Charles and Rebecca Ridgely, ca. 1770

Profits from his Northampton Ironworks during the Revolutionary War and from confiscated Loyalist properties afterward helped to fund Captain Ridgely's finest and most lasting achievement, the building of the "house in the forest" beginning in 1783.

2

The Building of Hampton
1783–1790

Work on the grand manor house at Hampton began as the Revolutionary War wound to a close. As the founding fathers strove to build the young republic of the United States, workers comprised of free craftsmen, indentured servants, and enslaved African-Americans labored to build Hampton Hall. Built between 1783 and 1790, it represented the culmination of Captain Ridgely's "American Dream." Hampton Hall stood as the centerpiece of the Northamp-

Historic American Buildings Survey drawing of Hampton Mansion, 1959

ton estate comprised of over eighteen thousand acres. Believed to be the largest private home in the country at that time, Hampton Hall served as a summer residence. Captain Ridgely also owned a house in Baltimore Town and another residential property on Patapsco Neck, in southeastern Baltimore County.

The Mansion cupola and Georgian architectural details

Construction of Hampton Hall began under the supervision of Jehu Howell (died 1787), a highly skilled builder and master carpenter referred to as "a very ingenious architect." The Mansion stands as one of the best surviving examples of Georgian architecture in the United States. The Georgian style, popular during the reigns of King George I, II, III, and IV of England, was inspired by classical revival buildings of the Italian Renaissance designed by Andreo Palladio. Captain Ridgely likely saw examples of Palladian architecture during his trips to England in the 1750s and early 1760s.

The winding stairs from the third floor to the cupola

During construction, the family lived in the Lower House or farmhouse, overseeing the work on the Mansion and the ironworks. Captain Ridgely supervised every phase of construction and closely scrutinized its cost. Ridgely manuscripts record the names of at least seventeen carpenters in addition to Howell who worked on the building of the house. Most of the exterior of the building, including the great "Doom" (the cupola)

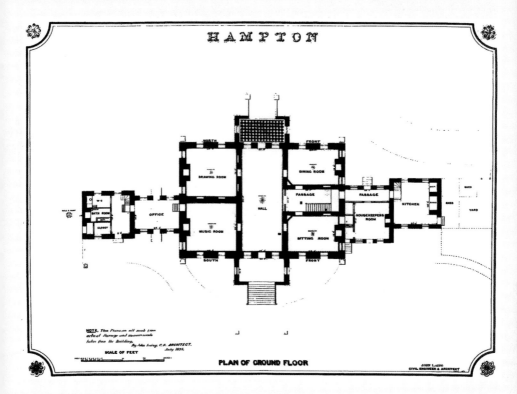

Floor plan of first floor of the Mansion by John Laing, 1875

and the vast shingled roof, and much of the interior woodwork had been completed by the time of Howell's tragic death from drowning in 1787. The Captain's wife Rebecca recorded moving to the "Large new dwelling" in December of 1788, although the interior of the house was not completely finished until 1790.

Modeled on the great country houses of Britain, Hampton's design follows a Palladian, symmetrical five-part plan: the main living space is located in the central block, connected to two service wings by "hyphens." Two-story porticoes adorn the north and south facades. The exterior was stuccoed and scored to look like stone, the pinkish buff color produced by the high iron content in the local sand. The enormous cupola on the roof and the Mansion's position on the hill reinforce the large size and importance of a structure that was designed to impress. A letter written in 1789 to Charles Ridgely was addressed "at Hampton Pallace." Unfortunately, Captain Ridgely, first owner and builder of Hampton Hall, did not long enjoy the fruits of his labor and died on June 28, 1790, shortly after the "pallace" was completed.

3

Hampton
1790–1829

The Hampton estate reached its zenith under Charles Carnan Ridgely (1760–1829), the second master. A nephew and principal heir of Captain Charles Ridgely, Charles Carnan Ridgely was the son of the Captain's sister Achsah and her husband, John Carnan. Trained in business by the Captain, Charles Ridgely Carnan eventually worked as his uncle's junior partner. He and Captain Ridgely maintained a close relationship. In 1782, Charles Ridgely Carnan married Priscilla Hill Dorsey (1762–

Engraved view of Hampton by William Russell Birch, 1808

1814), a younger sister of his uncle's wife, Rebecca. As primary heir to Captain Ridgely, Charles Ridgely Carnan with his wife and children took up residence in the Mansion at the same time as the Captain late in 1788.

Charles and Rebecca Ridgely had no children, and the Captain designated Charles Ridgely Carnan as his principal heir. By the terms of his uncle's will, Charles Ridgely Carnan inherited twelve thousand acres of land including the Hampton estate, two-thirds ownership of the Northampton Iron Furnace, other ironworks interests, and additional property, on the condition he change his surname to Ridgely, which he readily agreed to do. By an Act of the Maryland Legislature, November 5, 1790, Charles Ridgely Carnan, his son Charles, and all of their descendants adopted the surname of Ridgely. Captain Ridgely's will also established a "courtesy" entail to protect the core of the Hampton estate: Hampton Hall, gardens and grounds, and the Home Farm passed continuously to the eldest Ridgely son. This entail was scrupulously followed until the estate's transfer to the National Park Service in 1948.

Portrait of Governor Charles Carnan Ridgely, copy by C. G. Stapko after Thomas Sully

Portrait of Priscilla Dorsey Ridgely, copy after Rembrandt Peale

A man of many interests, Charles Carnan Ridgely expanded the Hampton estate. By the early nineteenth century he owned more than twenty-five thousand acres of land and three hundred enslaved people. While the ironworks continued to feed the family fortune, the ever-growing agricultural lands provided food for the workforce and the Ridgely family and some profit. Wheat, corn, and other grains comprised the primary crops. As president of the Maryland Agricultural Society, he advocated responsible use of land and wrote articles on crop rotation. He displayed his wealth and grandeur of his estate through his prize cattle, sheep, hogs, and championship Thoroughbred racehorses (see page 39). A British visitor noted, "The General's lands are very well cultivated . . . his

cattle, sheep, horses, etc., of a superior sort, and in much finer condition than many I saw in America."

Ridgely also played an active role in the business, political, and social life in Maryland. He served as a representative from Baltimore County in the Maryland Legislature from 1790 to 1795, as a state senator from 1796 to 1800, and as a three-term governor of Maryland from 1815 to 1818. Known throughout his life as General Ridgely, Charles Carnan Ridgely's military record culminated with his appointment as a brigadier general in the state militia in 1796.

A view of Hampton is featured on the crest rail of a Neoclassical painted chair, ca. 1805

A number of Charles Carnan Ridgely's improvements to the estate can be seen today. He completed the original plans for the formal gardens at Hampton, the landscaping of the north and south lawns, and construction of specialized garden structures. At the Mansion, he deepened the east hyphen allowing for direct access to the dining room and the addition of a servants' stair and continued to add fashionable interior finishes such as faux graining of the doors on the first floor.

Noted for his great hospitality, he was said to "keep the best table in America." One biographer wrote: "He had the fortune that enabled him to live like a prince, and he also had the inclination."

Charles Carnan and Priscilla Dorsey Ridgely had fourteen children, eleven of whom lived to maturity. Priscilla Ridgely died in 1814; their eldest son and presumed heir, Charles Carnan Ridgely, Jr., passed away on June 19, 1819, predeceasing his father. After an attack of paralysis, Charles Carnan Ridgely died in July 1829. By the terms of his will, many of his slaves were manumitted (freed). This manumission of over two hundred people was one of the largest in Maryland history. The Mansion and about forty-five hundred acres surrounding were bequeathed to John Carnan Ridgely (1790–1867), his second son, who became the new master of Hampton.

4

Hampton
1829–1867

J ohn Ridgely (1790–1867), the third master of Hampton, lived during an era of great social and political change nationwide. The industrial revolution, abolition of slavery, and the American Civil War profoundly changed the lifestyle and landscape of Hampton. The first child to be born at Hampton Hall, John's life was not marked by the ambition or prominence of Hampton's first two masters. He married his first wife Prudence Gough Carroll (1795–1822) in 1812. Prudence gave birth to six daughters, none of whom survived childhood. She died in 1822. In 1828,

Portrait of John Ridgely (detail) by Thomas Sully, 1841

John Ridgely married his second wife, Eliza Eichelberger Ridgely (1803–1867), only child of Nicholas Greenbury Ridgely (1770–1829), a prominent and very prosperous Baltimore merchant. Although the two believed they were distant cousins, no common descent for the two Ridgely

Right: Miniature portrait of Eliza Ridgely by G. L. Saunders, 1841

The Ridgely family barouche carriage, ca. 1840

Watercolor view of south façade of Hampton by Robert Carey Long, Jr., 1838 (private collection)

families has been established. They had five children, two of whom survived to adulthood, Eliza called "Didy" (1828–1894) and Charles (1830–1872).

When Governor Charles Carnan Ridgely died in 1829, the Hampton "empire" was reduced largely through division among eleven heirs. John Ridgely's inheritance of the Hampton estate encompassed only the courtesy entail of about forty-five hundred acres. Although the iron business continued to operate through the 1830s, advances in metallurgy and processing moved the industry to places such as Scranton and Pittsburgh. The Ridgelys' ironworks had ceased operation by 1850. Although the majority of the enslaved people at Hampton were manumitted by Governor Ridgely's will in 1829, John Ridgely purchased

The Cedar of Lebanon on the Great Terrace, planted in the 1830s

Silver ewer by J. A. Cressend, Paris, ca. 1822, presented to the Ridgelys by the Marquis de Lafayette

sixty-one more slaves and the practice continued at Hampton until 1864. In the decade before the Civil War, Hampton resembled more an agricultural plantation of the Deep South than a former industrial site.

John Ridgely never held public office; his interests were largely confined to his estate and its development and improvement. His greatest interest was "a great passion for horses and the outdoor life." In the social arena, John was eclipsed by his wife, Eliza, considered "one of the loveliest & most accomplished women ever raised in the city of Baltimore." Well educated by the standards of the day, Eliza spoke fluent French and Italian. An international traveler with very sophisticated taste, she was a friend of the Marquis de Lafayette, to whom she was introduced during his visit to Baltimore in 1824. At Hampton she became "the presiding spirit of the domestic circle ... wisely directing the work of the household and garden force. . . ." A noted horticulturist, her greatest passion was the garden, to which she "took a devoted interest ... [and]

Left: Carte de visite, a photographic calling card, of Eliza Ridgely III, c. 1862

Right: Portrait of Henry White, Julian White, John Ridgely, and Charles Ridgely at Hampton by John Carlin, 1856

was unsparing in her expenditures to improve them." Under her direction, most of the ornamental trees were planted about the grounds at Hampton, many of which have survived into the twenty-first century.

John and Eliza also took several extended tours of Europe, including in 1833–1834, 1846–1848, 1852, and 1859. In addition to adding extensively to the art collection and stylish furnishings of the Mansion, there were many improvements that "modernized" the house, including bathrooms and water closets, "central" heating provided by a hot-air furnace installed in the cellar, and the construction of a gas house to provide gaslight.

John, elderly at the time of the Civil War, had allowed his son Charles to manage Hampton since the mid-1850s. John and Eliza Ridgely died within a few months of each other in 1867.

Right: Daguerreotype of Eliza "Didy" Ridgely II with her husband John Campbell White, ca. 1849

The Civil War at Hampton

Located in a border state, Hampton witnessed the causes and effects of the American Civil War firsthand. The Ridgelys, with more than sixty-one slaves, were the second largest slave-owning family in Baltimore County in 1860. As the issues of slavery and economic dependency became more divisive in the mid-nineteenth century, their loyalties became divided and their way of life threatened. The industrial aspects of the Hampton estate had disappeared by 1850. With an agricultural base, the family was not inclined to support the industrial and commercial interests of free states to the North. Southern sympathizer James McHenry Howard summarized the family's dilemmas and anxieties: "Though both of them [John and Eliza] were . . . sympathetic with the South, yet their large interests in real estate, personal and slave property, and their knowledge that Maryland would be a buffer state between the contending sections; the dread of confiscation and possible slave insurrection . . . embittered to both of them, the years of the war. . . ."

Portrait of Charles Ridgely (detail) attributed to John E. Robertson, ca. 1868

In January 1861, a group of "state's rights gentlemen" established the Baltimore County Horse Guards, formally organized under Maryland's militia laws. Charles Ridgely (1830–1872), John and Eliza's son, was elected captain and chief officer of the cavalry company. Shortly after a pro-Confederate riot in Baltimore on April 19, 1861, the Horse Guards were sent to Whetstone Point outside Fort McHenry to guard against confrontation between Union troops and the citizens of the city. During the following days, the company patrolled the York Road to

James McHenry Howard in Confederate uniform, ca. 1863

Carte de visite of the north façade of Hampton, ca. 1861, the earliest photographic image of the house

David Ridgely Howard, Margaretta Howard Ridgely's half-brother, in Confederate uniform, ca. 1864

Cockeysville, followed retreating Union troops to the Pennsylvania border and received orders to destroy railroad bridges to the north. Captain Ridgely appointed Lieutenant John Merryman of "Hayfields" estate and other members of the Horse Guards to carry out that order.

On May 25, 1861, Lieutenant Merryman was arrested and taken to Fort McHenry. His arrest and subsequent disposition was the subject of Roger Brooke Taney's landmark U.S. Supreme Court opinion *ex parte Merryman*, dealing with the writ of habeas corpus. Charles Ridgely was never arrested, however. General John Dix of New York, in command of the U.S. troops in Baltimore and a personal friend of John Ridgely, informed John that a warrant had been issued for Charles's arrest. John assured General Dix that his son was not a conspirator against the United States and that he would remain quietly at Hampton for the balance of hostilities. The Baltimore County Horse Guard Company was disbanded.

Although the Hampton Ridgelys did not actively participate in the War after this time, they were still afflicted with the divided loyalties. John and Eliza's grandson Henry White recalled: "My grandfather always professed to be a 'Union man'; but it was not long before I noticed feelings of marked satisfaction whenever the Southerners won a victory." Eliza Ridgely's Eichelberger relations in Baltimore were mostly Union sympathizers, but "the harassment and worry of the Civil War were too much for [her]" and she lived in fear of a slave revolt. Charles Ridgely's brothers-in-law David and James McHenry Howard both served in the Confederate Army; David lost a leg and both escaped to Canada for a time. It is known that three Ridgely slaves managed to join the Union Army during the conflict. Following the abolition of slavery in Maryland in November 1864, only a handful of Hampton's previously enslaved individuals chose to stay on in employment.

5

Hampton
1867–1904

Hampton's fourth master Charles Ridgely (1830–1872) managed Hampton during the turbulent years after the American Civil War. Following the abolition of slavery in Maryland in 1864, many large estates went bankrupt. Charles Ridgely guided the Hampton estate from a slave-based labor force to one based on tenant farmers. His background reflects the life of an antebellum Southern gentleman.

Hand-colored photo of Charles Ridgely, ca. 1865

Charles was the second child of John and Eliza Ridgely. He received much of his early education at the highly regarded Mr. McNally's school in Baltimore and graduated from Harvard University. Receiving a classical education, he read Greek and Latin. In 1851 Charles returned to Hampton and married his first cousin Margaretta Sophia Howard (1824–1904), daughter of James and Sophia Ridgely Howard. Margaretta, affectionately known to the family as "Dumps," was a childhood playmate of Charles' sister "Didy." Margaretta and Charles resided at Hampton after the time of their marriage. Charles assumed the responsibility for managing both the estate and his parents' investments early on.

Charles and Margaretta had seven surviving children between 1851 and 1869: four sons (John, Charles, Howard, and Otho) and three daughters (Eliza, Juliana Elizabeth, and Margaretta Sophia). Only one of the daughters (Juliana, later Mrs. John Southgate Yeaton) married. Margaretta Sophia (1869–1949) eventually became a missionary to Liberia after her mother's death where she founded a school for girls (see page 48). Eliza (1858–1954) became a leader in the Baltimore philanthropic community and was a founder of the United Women of Maryland.

The Civil War (see page 25 for Charles' involvement) and subsequent deaths of both John and Eliza Ridgely in 1867 brought many changes to Hampton. Charles and Margaretta sent their elder sons, John and Charles, Jr., to Europe early in 1866 in the company of their aunt "Didy" who was "procuring for them all the best instruction," principally in Paris. In the summer of 1870, Charles, Margaretta, and the younger children followed. Charles, however, "loved his home with all his heart, in fact had an unusually strong attachment to it." Thus, despite his long absences from

Engraving of Hampton from Appleton's Journal, *1875*

HAMPTON. MARYLAND.

Hampton, Charles maintained an active correspondence with his estate manager and gardeners during his trip. This correspondence reveals dissatisfaction with the outcome of the Civil War. Sadly, Charles died of typhoid fever at the age of forty-two, on March 29, 1872, in Rome, Italy. Margaretta and their children returned to Hampton to begin another era.

The Hampton estate continued to face dramatic changes in the labor force, agricultural practices and production during the period of Reconstruction. Though in 1872 the property technically passed to its fifth master, Captain John Ridgely (1851–1938), under the terms of his father's will his mother Margaretta continued to manage the estate until her death in 1904. In the early 1880s, she expended funds on the last major maintenance campaign for the Mansion and grounds while the property remained in private ownership. The workforce of tenant farmers rented the land from the Ridgelys by sharing their crops or a direct money rent. The latter nineteenth century saw an overall decline in agricultural prices with the opening of the Transcontinental Railway. Facing a dwindling estate and a decline in profits from farming, John was required to assume more responsibility for managing Hampton by the end of the nineteenth century. Throughout this time, the Hampton cattle herds continued to be of primary importance to the farming operations, though horses also remained central in the family lifestyle.

Hand-colored photo of Margaretta Howard Ridgely, ca. 1865

Helen West Stewart Ridgely (1854–1929), the wife of Captain John Ridgely, had been born and raised in Baltimore, but she actually met her future husband while traveling in Europe in 1871. The couple married in 1873 and eventually had eight children together. Helen was a highly accomplished woman: a talented writer, antiquarian, artist, genealogist, manager, and hostess. She was the author of two books still considered standard references, *The Old Brick Churches of Maryland* (1894) and *Historic Graves of Maryland and the District of Columbia* (1908).

Pastimes

Margaretta Ridgely and Helen Ridgely at the Atlantic City Boardwalk, ca. 1895

Lady at drawing class, ca. 1895

John Ridgely, Jr., with bicycle, ca. 1895

Men playing croquet at Hampton, ca. 1895

Playing baseball at Hampton, ca. 1895

J. Walker Ridgely and John Ridgely III fishing, ca. 1918

Helen Morris Ridgely taking her photograph in a mirror, ca. 1895

Helen Ridgely writing, near her typewriter, ca. 1895

Gentleman playing a banjo, ca. 1895

D. Stewart Ridgely and cousin Margaret Yeaton playing at Hampton, ca. 1895

6

Hampton in the
Twentieth Century

Posthumous portrait of Captain John Ridgely by Corrie Crook, 1940

Always styled "Captain," John Ridgely (1851–1938) saw the changes in America and Hampton from the Civil War until the eve of World War II. He technically became the fifth master upon the death of his father Charles Ridgely in 1872, but his mother continued the actual management of the estate for many years afterward. John oversaw an estate that was both dwindling in size and in profitability by the early twentieth century. After the death of his mother, Margaretta, in 1904 and the division of the estate among several heirs, Captain John Ridgely inherited just one thousand acres including the Home Farm, the remaining entailed part of the estate. Known as a "gentleman farmer," Captain Ridgely left the actual farming work to others. John's wife Helen wrote in her diary that he spent his day "saunter[ing] around with his hands in his pockets leaving work to overseer and men."

In 1905, the Ridgelys sold their town house, then located in Baltimore's fashionable Bolton Hill neighborhood, and began year-round residence at Hampton. By then,

Hampton's lavish and elegant lifestyle had diminished and, although the estate was cared for, little change or improvement took place. Captain John's wife, Helen West Stewart Ridgely (1854–1929), managed the estate's dairy and agricultural production, and instituted practical changes to the gardens that required less maintenance. A friend of the Theodore Roosevelts, Helen in her diary chronicles the collecting of eggs from the chicken house at Hampton in the morning and dressing to catch the train to Washington for tea at the White House in the afternoon. She cherished the traditions at Hampton and was very interested in genealogy and the history of the estate. She refused to allow electricity to be installed in the Mansion, though it was she who drove an automobile, a modern convenience her husband disdained.

John Ridgely, Jr. (1882–1959), eldest son of Captain John and Helen

Left: Portrait of John Ridgely, Jr., by Stanislav Rembski, ca. 1950

Right: *Louise Humrichhouse Ridgely with her son John Ridgely III, ca. 1912*

Pastel portrait of Helen Ridgely by Florence Mackubin, 1904

Ridgely, eventually became the sixth and final master of the Hampton estate. After his marriage to Louise Roman Humrichhouse in 1907, he built a large house at 503 Hampton Lane, where he and his wife raised a family of three children, the oldest son being John Ridgely III (1911–1990). By the end of World War I, Baltimore's suburbs were growing toward the formerly remote estate, and farming in the area became increasingly less viable. After his mother Helen's death, John Ridgely, Jr., established the Hampton Development Company with the agreement of his father in 1929. The plan was to construct and sell houses on Hampton lands near the heart of the Home Farm. The Great Depression and subsequent World War forestalled the subdivision of the estate by fifteen years. When his wife Louise died in 1934, John Ridgely, Jr., moved back to Hampton Mansion.

In 1936, John Ridgely III and his wife, Lillian Ketchum (1912–1995), who had married the previous year, also moved to Hampton. The young Mrs. Ridgely undertook the arduous responsibilities of mistress of the house for three generations of John Ridgelys, all living together in the Mansion. She managed the household, maintained farm records, and was especially interested in the upkeep and improvements in the gardens. Captain John Ridgely died in 1938, having been master of the Hampton estate for sixty-six years, the property passing to John Ridgely, Jr., who was to be the estate's last private owner. In 1939, he married for a second time to Jane Rodney. John Ridgely III and Lillian then moved to the Lower House or farmhouse, the first Ridgelys to occupy it since the 1780s. They left the residence in 1942 when he served in the Pacific Theater in the Army Air Corps and she was commissioned a lieutenant in the Army Nurse Corps. By the time of their return to the estate following the war, major changes were in motion.

HAMPTON

A GROUP OF COUNTRY ~ ~ ~ ~ ~ ESTATES OVERLOOKING THE WATERS OF LOCH ~ ~ ~ ~ ~ RAVEN

The Hampton Company brochure, ca. 1929

7

Hampton Becomes a Unit
of the National Park Service

Portrait of Eliza Ridgely with the Harp, copy by C. G. Stapko after Thomas Sully

During the Great Depression, upkeep of the Mansion, its remaining grounds, farm, and outbuildings had become increasingly difficult for the Ridgelys. The high cost of maintenance and estate and property taxes led the family to sell some of its contents. John Ridgely, Jr., was worried that Hampton would be lost to the encroaching suburbs, the furnishings sold off piecemeal and the Mansion destroyed. Ironically, the estate was saved, indirectly, because of a single painting.

During the summer of 1945, David Finley, director of the National Gallery of Art, learned of the magnificent portrait of Eliza Ridgely, *Lady with a Harp*, by Thomas Sully. He visited Hampton to see the painting, hoping to acquire it for the museum's collection. Following negotiations with John Ridgely, Jr., the painting was purchased for the National Gallery and another important work by Sully, the 1822 portrait of Governor Charles Carnan Ridgely, was presented to the museum as a gift by Mr. and Mrs. Ridgely.

Returning to Washington, D.C., David Finley, who had been very impressed with Hampton and Mr. Ridgely's concerns for its preservation, discussed saving the estate with influential people including noted architectural historian Fiske Kimball, Mrs. Ailsa Mellon Bruce (National Gallery donor Andrew Mellon's daughter), Donald Shepard of the Avalon Foundation (Mrs. Bruce's family foundation), and Ronald Lee (chief historian of the National Park Service). After a lengthy period of review by the National Park Service, an agreement was reached with John Ridgley, Jr., to sell the Mansion, some of its furnishings, and 43.29 acres to the Avalon Foundation. Because of postwar budget problems, the National Park Service agreed to accept Hampton as a donation from the Avalon Foundation provided an organization could be found to manage the site. The Society for Preservation of Maryland Antiquities was appointed the custodian of the property through a cooperating agreement with the National Park Service,

John and Jane Ridgely leaving the Mansion, 1948 (photo: A. Aubrey Bodine)

The Drawing Room undergoing restoration, 1949

approved by President Harry Truman on October 6, 1947. The Secretary of the Interior officially designated Hampton a National Historic Site on June 22, 1948.

Hampton's preservation also became the impetus for the formation of the National Trust for Historic Preservation, organized by some of the same people who established the cooperative effort between government and private philanthropy in the saving of Hampton. This was the first instance in which the National Park Service acquired a historic property based on its "outstanding merits as an architectural monument," rather than for historic connections to famous events or individuals. Through additional funding from the Avalon Foundation, the Mansion was restored on both interior and exterior, and on May 2, 1950, the site was opened to the public. The Society for the Preservation of Maryland Antiquities served as the custodian of Hampton National Historic Site for the next thirty years.

John Ridgely, Jr., and his second wife, Jane Rodney, moved to the Lower House, which they enlarged by adding a four-room wing and modern conveniences. After John's death in 1959, his widow Jane retained life tenancy until her death in 1978. Recognizing its role in conveying the

Dedication of Hampton National Historic Site, April 30, 1950. Left to right: David Finley, director of the National Gallery of Art; William Preston Lane, Governor of Maryland; Robert Garrett, president of the Society for the Preservation of Maryland Antiquities; Newton Drury, director of the National Park Service

Aerial view of Hampton in 1953

full significance of the site, the National Park Service purchased the 14.02-acre Home Farm, including the Lower House (the oldest building on the Hampton estate), two Slave Quarters, the Dairy, Mule Barn, Long House Granary, and other outbuildings, from the Ridgely family heirs and assumed full management of the entire site. A new partner association, Historic Hampton, Inc., was established at this time as a private, nonprofit cooperative organization of volunteers to generate community support and to help expand and enhance the programs and interpretation of Hampton National Historic Site.

8

Aristocratic Tastes

Horses and Horseracing

Thoroughbred horses and horseracing have been a major part of the Hampton estate since its founding. References indicate that as early as 1745 Colonel Charles Ridgely actively served as a member of the newly founded Maryland Jockey Club and passed on his love of horses to his son, Charles the Builder. The racing and breeding of Thoroughbred horses at Hampton reached its height under second master Charles Carnan Ridgely, said in his day to be "very famous for race horses," but continued well into the twentieth century. Successful Ridgely horses such as Grey Medley, Tuckahoe, and Bonaparte enhanced the wealth and fame of their owners. Horseracing had important social implications. Owning racehorses attested to a family's status as "landed gentry" while betting at races measured one's appetite for risk. Racing matches were frequently attended by leading businessmen, politicians, military heroes, and even presidents while many jockeys were enslaved African-Americans.

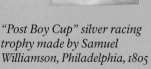

"Post Boy Cup" silver racing trophy made by Samuel Williamson, Philadelphia, 1805

Expenses related to maintaining Thoroughbreds were considerable. Records at Hampton indicate that a prize racehorse could cost three times the amount of a slave,

The Elkridge Hunt on the front lawn of Hampton, 1909

and ten times the amount of an average workhorse. Jockeys were provided with an elaborate silk jacket, cap, boots, and customized buttons, usually sporting the family crest. Two large horse stables, one dating from 1805 and the second from 1857, illustrate the longstanding importance of horses to the site. To keep horses in practice, the Ridgelys had their own private racetrack located within view of the Mansion. Hampton's third master John Ridgely favored expensive carriage horses and was renowned for driving carriages at "full speed," whereby he "was accustomed to do the distance from the City to Hampton [ten miles] in an hour or less." The close affinity of the Ridgelys to their horses may best be summed up with the following memoir describing John's death in 1867: "Only one or two days before his death, he caused his favourite riding horse, Satin, to be brought up to the house and gazing from the

Wager for $10,000 related to Post Boy, 1809

dining room window he admired his glossy shining coat and said 'Ah old fellow, I am afraid I shall never ride you again'. . . and sadly ordered him to be taken back to the stable."

The Ridgelys and other leading families like them established the longstanding equestrian tradition that Maryland still enjoys to this day. Foxhunting and steeplechase racing have long been key parts of this tradition, and the Ridgelys were active participants in both in the late nineteenth and early twentieth centuries. Meets of the Elkridge Hunt Club were held frequently at Hampton during the 1880s to 1910s, and the Maryland Hunt Cup, a renowned steeplechase race considered one of the most difficult in the world, was run at Hampton four times (1895, 1903, 1919, and 1920).

Post Boy, "the great Maryland Horse"

Of all the racehorses owned by the Ridgelys, none was more famous than Post Boy. Purchased by Charles Carnan Ridgely in 1803 as a young colt, he won nearly every race for the next six years. Post Boy won purses of $500 to $1,000 in races held in Baltimore, Richmond, Alexandria, and other major cities. Post Boy's fame was so great that in 1809 a $10,000 bet was proposed that Post Boy would beat Potomac at the Washington City Jockey Club Race Course during the following October. Sadly, the race never took place as Post Boy broke his leg in a heated race two weeks prior to the proposed meet.

Foxhunters and their hounds near Hampton, ca. 1915

Louise Humrichhouse Ridgely on horseback, 1912

41

Entertaining at Hampton

Within the doors I found true hospitality where I am informed it has long presided; . . . assembled in the spacious apartments of this palace, a constellation of grace, wit and beauty not to be excelled. . . . The entertainments were all social and intellectual; presenting a fine opportunity to grow in knowledge and grace. . . . The repast was such as refinement alone could prepare, consisting of the richest viands.
—1832 newspaper account of a dinner at Hampton

From the very beginning, guests at Hampton were entertained with great style and graciousness. The earliest recorded case of entertaining at the Mansion dates from the late 1780s when the Ridgely family had just moved in, described about a century later by memoirist James McHenry Howard. "When the house warming of the present family mansion took place it was kept differently up stairs from what it was below. Down stairs Rebecca the wife of the Captain [Charles Ridgely the Builder]

The Dining Room set for dinner in the manner of ca. 1820

& who was a good old-fashioned Methodist inaugurated her housewarming by religious services and a watch meeting in the large-hall, while her husband the Captain had a card party with its usual accompaniments above stairs."

Hampton continued to host grand entertainments under Governor Charles Carnan Ridgely, who was said to "keep the best table in America." British visitor and travel writer Richard Parkinson in 1805 further commented, "I often experienced his great hospitality." The Governor's parties could be quite large, as his friend Henry Thompson recorded in his diary in 1812, "Fifty one People sat down to Dinner in the Hall and had plenty of room." To provide for such a feast, the Hampton estate would have been self-sufficient in terms of meat (beef, poultry, pork), fish, eggs, fruit (apples, pears), vegetables, grains, nuts, and dairy products. In addition, the Ridgely wine cellar was extensive and able to amply supply guests.

Bottle of Hampton Madeira wine, "Rainwater," 1815

Lavish parties could cost a small fortune and involved large quantities of food. In 1840, the list of provisions for a party for hundreds of guests included six dozen chickens, three hundred hard crabs, five dozen bottles of champagne, and a cake so large it required six dozen eggs! The wedding receptions of John and Eliza's children Didy and Charles in 1849 and 1851 respectively were equally large with very bountiful fare. Even smaller parties during this

A garden party at Hampton in 1916, attended by President and Mrs. Theodore Roosevelt

era were extremely elegant. Elizabeth Wirt Goldsborough wrote her sister the following description of her visit to Hampton in 1848: "She [Eliza] had prepared a sumptuous dinner. . . . Everything was served up in European style—splendid china, glass, silver & a succession of courses, variety of wines—and everything beautifully garnished with flowers—and she sat at the head of her table—like a Queen—full of animated conversation & amiable attention to everybody."

Even with dwindling fortunes, there were still opulent special events held at Hampton in the early twentieth century. In 1916, John and Helen Ridgely hosted a large garden party for their friends, the Theodore Roosevelts. Photos in family albums show hundreds of elegantly attired guests strolling the grounds. Another festive occasion for John and Helen was the celebration of their fiftieth wedding anniversary in 1923. Guests brought lavish gifts including several gold plated vases and other decorative items still in Hampton's collection. One of the last parties held at Hampton during the Ridgely era was the debutant party in 1943 for Margie Whitham, hosted by her mother's first cousin John Ridgely, Jr., last private owner of Hampton. The photos of Baltimore society figures who attended were prominently featured in the local newspaper.

Visitors to Hampton

In the close to 160 years that the Ridgely family lived at Hampton, hundreds if not thousands of people came to visit. Some stayed a few hours, others for days, and in some instances months. One of the earliest well-known guests was famed British agriculturalist Richard Parkinson, who visited Charles Carnan Ridgely at Hampton in the late 1790s. Parkinson arrived in the United States in 1798 and for the next three years traveled around the United States observing the agricultural practices of American farmers. During his tour he was introduced to Ridgely and stayed for some days at Hampton observing the farming techniques employed. Parkinson later recounted his

Carte de visite of distinguished British visitor Lady Georgina Fane, ca. 1861

Invitation to a dinner in honor of noted diplomat Henry White, 1910

acquaintance with Ridgely in his book *A Tour of America, 1798–1800*, where he commented, "The General's lands are very well cultivated . . . his cattle, sheep, horses, etc., of a superior sort, and in much finer condition than many I saw in America."

John Carnan Ridgely and Eliza Eichelberger Ridgely entertained frequently at Hampton. As a family member observed, "Mrs. John Ridgely & her husband exercised a wide hospitality during their possession of Hampton, & there was seldom a time when there was not some guest more or less distinguished staying at that place." Three English visitors stood out in his memory: the Marquess of Hartington, later the eighth Duke of Devonshire; Colonel Charles Powell Leslie III; and Lady Georgina Fane. Lord Hartington and Colonel Leslie both visited Hampton in the winter of 1862 and 1863 and spent some time ducking at Carroll's Island. Lady Georgiana, famous in England for her relationship with the Duke of Wellington, expressed a deep interest in the treatment of the enslaved African-Americans during her visit to Hampton and was given the freedom to visit their quarters.

John and Eliza's grandson Henry White was a diplomat and described by President Theodore Roosevelt as "the most useful man in the entire diplomatic service, during my Presidency and for many years before." Henry, who spent much of his childhood at Hampton, commented that it "was a place to which all foreigners of distinction who visited this country were brought as a matter of course." Notable visitors who accompanied Henry included a December 1906 visit by First Lady Edith Kermit Roosevelt; noted Senator Henry Cabot Lodge; and Signor des Planches, the Italian Ambassador in Washington, D.C.

Well traveled, educated, and politically and socially connected, the Ridgelys were host to other notable guests including Le Comte de Heussenstam Chamberlaine from the Austrian Court who came to visit in 1903. Former missionary Margaretta S. Ridgely, daughter of Charles and Margaretta, invited Walter Henry Overs, the Bishop of Liberia and an African chief, to visit in 1924.

Noblesse Oblige

Beyond the halls of Hampton many members of the Ridgely family supported charitable causes by which they were inspired. Ranging from religious charities to public works, the Ridgely women especially found themselves active in the philanthropic scene in Baltimore and, in some instances, the world.

Religion played a very large role in the philanthropic acts in which the various generations of the Ridgely family participated. First mistress of Hampton, Rebecca Dorsey Ridgely, a devout convert to Methodism, arranged for the renowned traveling minister Robert Strawbridge to have a residence on one of the properties owned by her husband, Captain Charles Ridgely.

Miniature portrait of Sophia Gough Ridgely, ca. 1815

Second owner Charles Carnan Ridgely was an incorporator of the Baltimore Orphan Asylum. Even more significant was the manumission through his will of over two hundred slaves, an act which family tradition ascribed to the influence of his pious Methodist daughter Sophia Gough Ridgely Howard.

John Carnan and Eliza Ridgely provided the financial backing and the stone for the construction of the Trinity Episcopal Church, purchased Bible Society certificates, and helped aid the Orphans Asylum. Eliza Ridgely also was involved with the welfare and religious education of the family's slaves and made significant donations to a wide variety of religious and charitable organizations that assisted the needy. She also meticulously recorded in her account books the numerous small gifts to poor individuals she met in daily life.

Eliza Ridgely III, ca. 1895

Eliza "Didy" Ridgely White Buckler became heavily involved with the education of young women. A highly educated woman herself and well traveled, Didy opened a girls' school in Warrington, Virginia, with the mission of educating girls from good Southern homes. On her various European travels as an adult, Didy took with her

young ladies from "distressed southern families" for education. After her son Julian's death, her home "The Causeway" was given to the Episcopal Church and turned into a convent.

Didy's nieces Margaretta and Eliza Ridgely III were both actively involved in large philanthropic projects. Margaretta is best known for her missionary work in Liberia and the founding of an Episcopal girls' school, a descendant of which survives to this day. Instead of collecting her salary as a missionary, she redirected the funds to support the efforts of a missionary in China. Her sister Eliza was more active locally in Baltimore, as a founder of the United Women of Maryland and as a board member of the Female House of Refuge. Particularly concerned with the welfare of disadvantaged women and children, Eliza was proactive in cleaning up public parks and building playgrounds for underprivileged city youth.

Photo of Margaretta S. Ridgely with tenant farmers' children, ca. 1895

Award from the Government of Liberia to Margaretta S. Ridgely, 1927

Helen Ridgely, the fifth mistress of Hampton and a sister-in-law to Eliza and Margaretta, was also active in church-related charitable activities. On a grander scale, she hosted a lawn fete in support of the Red Cross during World War I.

Perhaps the greatest philanthropic act by the Ridgely family was the selling of the Mansion and part of the collection to the Avalon Foundation at far below market value in 1948. By choosing to do this, John Ridgely, Jr., enabled the core of the estate, buildings, and collections to be preserved for future generations.

Heraldry at Hampton

One of the most striking features a visitor sees while touring the Mansion is the prolific use of the Ridgely coat of arms. Although such heraldic devices are more common among European aristocracy, they can be found among some prominent American families. Often, a coat of arms symbolizes social stature, as well as family alliances. These symbols of status and family distinction became an essential part of the Ridgely family's environment. Indeed, perhaps nowhere in Maryland was the use of a family coat of arms more widespread than at Hampton.

Charles Ridgely Carnan was named as Captain Charles Ridgely's principal heir under the condition he change his surname to Ridgely. This was accomplished by an act of the Maryland Legislature in 1790. Ridgely and his descendants were also granted the right "to use and bear the coat of arms and armorial bearings of the family of Ridgely," described as "argent on a chevron sable three mullets pierced of the first."

Gilded wall mirror with Ridgely crest by Samson Cariss, 1851

The earliest extant example of the Ridgely coat of arms at Hampton is the heraldic shield on several pieces of silver

ordered by Charles Carnan Ridgely in the early 1790s. These include a large set of graduated salvers by Standish Barry and a tea caddy by William Ball, both leading Baltimore silversmiths. The shield alone was also used on the massive pair of gilded pier mirrors and matching cornices made for the Drawing Room in ca. 1843 (see pages 84–85).

Much more frequently, the family used the shield with the "buck's head erased" (stag's head) crest or just the crest alone. Most of Hampton's silver flatware and hollowware made in the nineteenth century was embellished with the crest, including wine coolers, butter dishes, a cruet stand, soup tureens, dish domes, and platters of all sizes. An ornate repoussé tea service by Samuel Kirk, probably purchased for Eliza Ridgely when she married in 1828, is similarly engraved. The family crest also ornaments the tea service made for the 1907 marriage of John Ridgely, Jr., and Louise Humrichhouse. Charles Carnan Ridgely's porcelain dinner service ordered in the 1820s from Feuillet of Paris has both shield and crest, while an English porcelain dessert service of the same date made by the Coalport factory has only the stag's head.

Cast gilt brass stag's head curtain tie-back by Samson Cariss, 1845

The use of the crest is found on objects ranging in size from a barouche carriage to small buttons on servants' livery, from stained-glass windows in the Great Hall to stationery, from cast-iron entrance gates to pocket handkerchiefs. Stag's heads embellished Hampton hall chairs, curtain tie-backs, window cornices, wall plaques, horse harnesses, letter openers, book plates, paper weights, cuff links, manicure sets, chamber sticks, table linens, bath towels, and crocheted afghans, to give but a few examples.

Armorial Paris porcelain sweetmeat dish by Feuillet, ca. 1825

English plated silver wine coolers with Ridgely crest, ca. 1825

9

The Workforce
at Hampton

Captain Charles Ridgely, his father and brother John all made a living from the operations at the Northampton Iron Works and later the Nottingham Iron Works. Eighteenth-century iron production was labor intensive and required many workers. The Ridgelys like many of their contemporaries used a mix of labor comprising enslaved African Americans, paid free laborers, and white indentured servants. Between 1750 and 1800 at least three hundred white servants toiled in the various entrepreneurial endeavors at the Northampton Iron Works and its supporting industries.

Illustration of the interior of an eighteenth-century iron furnace

Indentured Servants at Hampton

Too poor to pay for transportation, men and women sold their labor for the price of ships passage from England to the Colonies and entered into an indenture agreement. By the time the Northampton Iron Works began buying indentured servants, a large portion of whom were convicts, they traded hard labor and

Indenture agreement between Charles Ridgely and Darby Kelly, 1770

passage for a fresh start in the New World when their contract was over.

An indenture contract included length of service, what provisions were to be extended to the indenture during his/her period of labor, and what the indenture's freedom dues were. Terms of service typically were for between four to six years for non-convict laborers and seven to fourteen years for convict laborers. Provisions included "meat, drink, apparel, washing, and lodging." Men at the furnace received one of each of the following per annum: jacket, breeches, shirt, stockings, shoes, hat, and blanket, plus one-half of a bed tick per person.

Indentured servants in general were white males and therefore recognized by the courts. The ability to pursue grievances in a court of law was a right not afforded to enslaved African Americans who worked alongside of indentured servants. Indentures at the Iron Works went to court twenty-eight times in 1788 alone.

The workday for indentured servants at the furnace is unclear; however time-books for the colliers (charcoal producers) exist. Colliers were expected to work twenty-six days per month, with only Sundays off. The workday likely started at sunup and ended when the sun went down or it became too dark to see. During slack times at the furnace, indentured servants were expected to serve as farmers and provide sustenance to their fairly isolated community. Indentures and slaves worked as smithies, smelters, tailors, weavers, and shoemakers. Felling trees, extracting ore and coal, hauling fuel, and moving finished products to port were additional jobs held by indentures.

Not surprising with the hard labor, long hours, and few breaks, indentures often ran away. Runaways that were captured and returned often found themselves not only subject to physical punishment but also to extensions on their terms of service. Not all indentures seemed to be running away to seek freedom. One individual, John Dehoddy, ran away at least seven times between 1772 and October 1777, when he received his freedom dues. Many of his forays away from the furnaces seemed only to serve as a break from the labor, on most occasions he returned on his own accord and was treated indulgently by the furnace managers.

The Enslaved at Hampton

Slave labor provided the backbone of the workforce at Hampton for over one hundred years. Like every place where slavery was practiced, the story of the enslaved is specific to the location while containing some commonalities of the "peculiar institution." Slavery at Hampton changed over time, following national trends and reflecting differing personal styles of Hampton's owners and overseers. The enslaved community of Hampton was a dynamic and diverse one and in some ways, a culture to themselves.

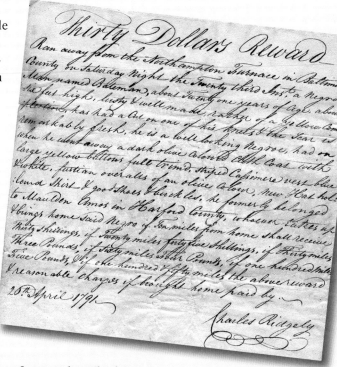

Work and discipline were regulated by one or more overseers and treatments varied. For example, one Nelson Cooper, overseer from 1845 to 1857 was described as "a very cruel manager and a bad man," whereas Charles Howard, was described as "a strict disciplinarian, yet the negroes were all fond of him."

Announcement of reward offered by Charles Carnan Ridgely for the return of the slave Bateman, 1791

CHRISTMAS GIFTS of the Colored Children of Hampton, given by E. Ridgely.

List of Christmas gifts given to enslaved children at Hampton, 1841–1854

The earliest references to slaves owned by the Ridgely family occur in 1747. While indentured servants constituted the majority of the labor force at that time, early records of slave labor at Hampton show that they were instrumental in clearing land for agricultural production and in the production of iron. Of the 130 slaves owned by the Ridgelys during the American Revolution, 30 worked directly in the Northampton Iron Furnace with 100 performing agricultural work that supported the workforce. Certain slaves held skilled and important positions. For example, one individual named "Toby" and another named "Daniel" held positions as "founder" at the Iron Works. They kept the furnace at peak efficiency, monitored the fire, smoke, and iron in the furnace and supervised the mix of raw ingredients. Their skills and position likely made them more valuable to the Ridgely family than the many indentured servants and paid laborers.

Former Slave Quarters at Hampton Home Farm, ca. 1895

The production of iron and need for slave labor at Northampton and other furnaces acquired by the Ridgely family remained high until the 1820s. Advances in metallurgy and the depletion of woodland led to the close of the furnaces decades later. Slaves continued to work as domestic servants in the Mansion and in agriculture until 1864.

Family life for the enslaved centered around the Slave Quarters. Existing cabins onsite are made of stone and date to about 1855, however records dating back to 1798 describe cabins of log construction, one as small as ten by twelve feet; another measured twenty-two by thirty-two feet. The later stone structures at Hampton are more substantial and commodious than quarters on most other plantations of the time (see page 61). Highly detailed records kept by Eliza Ridgely (1803–1867) show the individual allotments of clothing, bedding, and other necessities supplied to the enslaved workers twice a year.

Former slave Nancy Davis with Eliza Ridgely III, ca. 1862

The number of people enslaved at Hampton varied over time. Immediately after the American Revolution slaveholding in Maryland surpassed indentured servitude, and Hampton was no exception. The number of slaves at Hampton would continue to rise until 1829 when the population numbered approximately 339. Ironically, during this same year, one of the largest manumissions in Maryland history took place at Hampton. Upon his death, Charles Carnan Ridgely manumitted (freed) many of his enslaved population. His son, inheriting a diminished estate both in workforce and in acreage, purchased approximately 60 people, a number that varied little at Hampton until the abolition of slavery in Maryland in 1864.

Tenant Farmers at Hampton

Like the curtain rising on a new drama, the abolition of slavery in Maryland on November 1, 1864, set the stage for a new era at Hampton. The time of slavery was over, and tenant farming had begun. Farm tenancy changed not

Tenant farmers near the corncrib on the Hampton Home Farm, ca. 1895

only the relationship between worker and owner but the very landscape of the estate itself. Unlike similar estates, the family fortune was large enough to enable the Ridgelys to weather the storms of declining agricultural prices, competition from the Midwest, and a shortage of labor for the next eighty years.

The years immediately following the American Civil War were marked by the transition from a slave-based labor force to tenancy. While some of the former Ridgely slaves left Hampton immediately after emancipation, a number remained. Like many former slaves in Maryland, they had little to bargain with over their hiring conditions, opportunities to work elsewhere were limited, and monthly wages were low—usually $8 to $10 and board.

Margaretta S. Ridgely with tenant farmers' children, ca. 1895

While the Ridgely fortune was substantial during the post–Civil War era, hiring laborers to work the entire estate was not economically feasible. Like many similar plantations, the estate was subdivided and worked by hundreds of tenant farmers. As a result, the landscape was physically changed. The formerly vast fields of corn and wheat now resembled a patchwork quilt of more numerous smaller plots, each worked by an individual family. A visiting journalist in 1889 stated: "Some 7,000 acres of land are included, of which all but a thousand are let to tenants. . . ."

At Hampton, tenant relationships were based on year-to-year individual contracts that were either "share rents," in which the Ridgelys received a portion of the produce from each rented farm, or "money rents," in which they were paid an annual rent in cash. Given the seasonal nature of farming, this system enabled farmers to reimburse the Ridgelys after the harvest. A farm manager was paid to oversee the tenants, the farm's livestock, agricultural production, and sales.

Former Slave Quarters in use for tenant housing, ca. 1895

Hampton was not immune to the problems experienced throughout Maryland regarding the shortage of available labor and declining agricultural prices. Letters between the Ridgely family and the farm manager indicate the difficulty in attracting reliable tenants and problems in collecting the annual rent in a timely manner. Conversely, tenants complained of unreasonable rents and unpredictability of annual harvests.

Tenant farming was a barely profitable endeavor for both tenant and landowner. However, despite poor profits, the farm appeared to be a well-organized system. A visitor in 1875 described Hampton as having "fertile, open fields, showing careful cultivation and well-limed soil. . . . there is a look of stability, adaptedness and antiquity." The end of the Home Farm as an agricultural unit began in 1929 with the establishment of the Hampton Development Company, although hired workers continued to work the Hampton fields in a limited capacity until the early 1950s.

Paid Staff at Hampton

From the time of the Mansion's construction in the 1780s till the day the Ridgelys moved out in 1948, the family relied on the talent and skills of many paid individuals. In 1783 Jehu Howell was hired as the master carpenter/architect for Hampton. Surviving ledger books from the Mansion's construction reflect payments to workmen who assisted in various aspects of building the Mansion, including no less than seventeen skilled carpenters plus turners, plasterers, painters, and glaziers.

Professional gardeners at work in Parterre II, 1879

Mr. Naylor the blacksmith and wheelwright, ca. 1890

The gardens and grounds at Hampton were extremely important to the Ridgely family, and the job of head gardener was highly regarded and well-paid. One gardener, whose name is unknown, was distinguished by his red leather shoes and his residence in the Mansion. In the mid-nineteenth century, Eliza Ridgely hired professional gardeners from out of state to supervise numerous improvements to the grounds. By the 1850s, the work of several paid under-gardeners (usually three in number) mostly supplanted slave labor in maintaining the grounds and orchards.

Another well-regarded position was that of cook, who was not only responsible for preparing lavish meals but also managing the kitchen and the enslaved kitchen workers. At one point the family had a skilled French chef hired by Charles

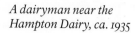

A dairyman near the Hampton Dairy, ca. 1935

Carnan Ridgely. Eliza Ridgely also employed specialized caterers and French pastry chefs when hosting parties for hundreds of guests.

The Ridgelys were the masters of Hampton, but the day-to-day management on the estate fell to the overseer. Often caught between the demands of the master and the needs of the workers, Hampton's overseers were a diverse group of men who stayed about ten years on the estate. Late eighteenth-century tax records indicate that Charles Carnan Ridgely needed several different individuals to oversee the activities on the various farms that comprised his vast landholdings. Later, Charles Ridgely Howard, nephew of the third master John Carnan Ridgely, worked as the overseer of the Home Farm and was regarded by his Uncle John to have managed the farm exceptionally well. After the Civil War, the Ridgelys hired farm managers to supervise farming operations.

Mary the cook by the octagonal building, which was used as servants quarters, 1936

Generations of the Ridgely children were raised with the help of governesses and tutors. Eliza "Didy" Ridgely often wrote about her governess Miss Kingsworth and her sister's nursemaid Mrs. Brown. Charles Ridgely employed private tutors who were responsible for preparing his sons for university. Tutors were also hired to provide art, music, and dancing lessons for the children.

An estate as large as Hampton required the work of dozens of individuals. Except for those few people who garnish a story or provide a side note in a ledger or memoir, the stories of many of the indentured, enslaved, and paid professional labor go untold.

10

Structures
on the Estate

T he many outbuildings surrounding the historic home and farm complex are a defining feature of Hampton's landscape. Combining both function and aesthetics, these rare survivors reflect the agricultural and leisure pursuits of the Ridgely family. Most of the outbuildings on the farm side date from the 1840s until 1860, a period of major renovations to the Home Farm and a classic example of the *ferme ornée* or ornamental farm. Popular in Europe, *ferme ornée* blended the practical with the aesthetic. Visually, it gave the impression of a small village. Practically, buildings were built primarily out of stone, were decorated with bargeboard (which assisted in water dissipation) and clustered according to use.

The Lower House, begun ca. 1745 with several later additions

The Lower House

Once the center of a twenty-three-hundred-acre tract, the Home Farm represented the core of the Ridgely family's agricultural operation. Overlooking the many outbuildings was the Lower House. For over two hundred years the Ridgely family added to, altered and adjusted the interior and exterior of this building. The entire history of the Hampton estate can be traced through changes made to the Lower House.

The earliest section of the Lower House dates to about 1745 and was likely one of many buildings that comprised a large tobacco plantation. The building was expanded during the 1760s and served as a residence while the Ridgely family visited the Iron Works and later during the building of the Mansion. During the early nineteenth century the Lower House served as an overseer's office and quarters. Following the abolition of slavery, it housed the farm manager.

In keeping with Ridgely traditions of entertaining, the building was known as the "Huntsman's Lodge" in the early twentieth century and served house guests attending fox-hunting events held during the fall and winter. The last addition to the Lower House was made in 1948 when John Ridgley, Jr., and his wife, Jane Rodney Ridgely, moved back in after selling the Mansion to the Avalon Foundation. Modern amenities were installed and the Lower House was known as the Ridgely House until the death of Jane in 1978.

The Slave Quarters

The former Slave Quarters, ca. 1855, behind the Lower House

Standing immediately behind the Lower House are two Slave Quarters (also see pages 54 and 57). Constructed circa 1855 out of stone cut from the Ridgley quarry, the Quarters were the center of slave family life. It is uncertain how many people lived in these dwellings. At the time of their construction, the number of enslaved people at Hampton numbered sixty-one, and there were other Slave Quarters, mainly built of wood, elsewhere on the property. A fascinating feature of these buildings is the walnut graining (faux painting) present on the interior woodwork that is similar to that found in the Music Room of the Mansion, grained in 1854. Paint analysis dates the graining in the Quarters to the time of construction in the mid-1850s.

The Stables

There are two two-story stone stables on the estate, dating from 1805 and 1857, which once housed some of the finest Thoroughbred horses in Maryland history, including Governor Charles Carnan Ridgely's favorite champion, Post Boy (see page 44). These stables are unusually large and well-built and reflect the family's love for their horses.

Stables I (1805) on right and Stables II (1857) seen through the meadow

The Mule Barn

The Mule Barn dates from the early 1850s

Located just northwest of the Lower House and adjacent to the cornfield, the Mule Barn (built ca. 1855) housed the primary work animals of the Home Farm. Used much as tractors are today, mules pulled plows, mowers, and other farm equipment at Hampton until the early twentieth century. The Ridgelys took great pride in their prize mules and frequently entered them in livestock competitions.

The Long House Granary

Constructed ca. 1855, the Long House Granary was built for the storage of wheat and other grains. The low openings at the base of this building suggest its use for hogs and related livestock. A very large stone "cow house" once stood nearby to the north.

Tenant farmers' children on the steps of the Long House Granary, ca. 1895

The Dairy

Built around 1790 over a natural spring, the Dairy served as the primary storage area for milk and the processing of butter. Milk was cooled by placing stoneware milk pails in a basin of water. In addition to milk storage, butter-production provided another source of income for the Ridgelys in the early nineteenth century. A newspaper account, published in *The American Farmer*, indicates that the estate made over $1,700 per year in 1822. The Dairy remained in use until the early 1940s.

Below left: The Dairy (ca. 1790) is among the earliest surviving outbuildings

Below right: Booklet recording John Ridgely's prize herd of Jersey dairy cows, 1882

The Corncrib

The wooden Corncrib (see page 56), built around 1855, was destroyed in a tragic fire in 1988. The foundation can still be seen today, and its large size attests to the dominance of corn as a crop at the Hampton estate. Once harvested, corn was stored in the Corncrib to air dry before it would be ground into cornmeal. Corn, the most widely grown crop in the United States, was consumed by both livestock and people.

The Log Cabin

Once thought to be a slave cabin, this building housed the blacksmith Charles Budd by 1908. Archeological investigations have not found any items predating emancipation, however, architectural evidence strongly suggests that the structure may have been constructed of salvaged remains of two previous farm buildings, possibly slave cabins. Newspaper from 1862 was identified in the daubing between the pine log chinks.

Outbuildings Near the Mansion

Eighteenth-century houses lacked the amenities found in homes today such as central heat, electric lights, and indoor plumbing. The Mansion was no exception, and

The octagonal building (ca. 1855), used as servants quarters, burned in the 1940s

with only a few rooms dedicated to service within the main structure, numerous outbuildings were required to support the family and their guests.

Located within the immediate vicinity of the Mansion are the domestic service buildings. Abutting the east wing or kitchen wing is the kitchen terrace, the octagonal building foundation (modern herb garden), and the Pump House. Historically in the mid-Atlantic a summer kitchen was erected. This provided a wonderful alternative to cooking indoors during the heat of the summer when standing over a fire was hot enough already. The Pump House, at the edge of the kitchen terrace, was built in the 1890s to house the pumping equipment for a gravity-fed water system that once supplied running water to the Mansion. The structure is now used for storage. Domestic servants were once housed in the octagonal building, which burned in the 1940s.

The automobile Garage east of the Mansion, ca. 1918

The Garage was constructed around 1910 and housed the family automobile. Fifth mistress Helen Ridgely was the first family member to drive, so it was most likely built for her car. Next to the Garage stands the former Paint Shed and Woodshed. These two buildings served various functions over the years and now appear as modified in the twentieth century. Missing service structures in this general area included a Carpenter's Shed, Smokehouse, Washhouse, and Cider Cellar.

Indoor plumbing was a luxury that the builder of Hampton did not have. Located just beyond the Garage and the Sheds are the two Privies that were used by family and guests as toilet facilities. Privies (short for privacy) were constructed close enough to the house to make their use convenient, but far enough away so that odors and other "unpleasantries" were kept at a distance. These privies both have hinged doors that run the length of the rear wall from which chamber pots placed inside could be removed.

Illustration of the Ice House, original to the 1790s

No longer standing except for its stone foundation is the Gas House. Prior to 1929, Hampton was lighted with gas that was produced on-site from coal and pumped into pipes that supplied the Mansion's lighting fixtures. This system, first installed in the 1850s, continued in use until after the death of Helen Ridgely in 1929, when Captain John Ridgely had electricity at last installed.

A dependency sometimes seen on country estates, Hampton's Ice House is unusual because it is larger and deeper than the average commercial ice pits. It was built to survive for generations with a stone-lined shaft and brick dome. Built around 1790 the Ice House is thirty-three feet seven inches deep and has a finely laid brick dome with a fieldstone wall.

The Family Cemetery

"And the day will come when the vaults of Hampton shall give up their dead," said Dr. Cole, Methodist minister, Epsom Chapel, at the conclusion of a eulogy given for Julia Ridgely, daughter of the third master, John Carnan Ridgely. Julia died before her fourth birthday. Located within walking distance of the Mansion, the family cemetery still stands today as a quiet resting place much as it has for the past two hundred years. The centerpiece of the cemetery is the family vault, built in the early nineteenth century. A rare example of Egyptian Revival architecture, it houses the remains of generations of Ridgely masters, mistresses, and other family members.

The headstones reflect various architectural styles from Gothic to Celtic and provide insight into the people who lived at Hampton. For example, the stone for Margaretta Sophia Howard Ridgely, founder of a girls' school in Liberia, Africa, states that she was called "Meissie," meaning "our mother," by her students. The marker for housekeeper Selina Devlin is inscribed "a friend of the family for eighty-four years." John Ridgley III, veteran of World War II and son of Hampton's last master, was known to joke with close friends that he wished to be buried near the cem-

The Ridgely Family Crypt, dating from the early nineteenth century, seen through the iron cemetery gates

etery entrance "in case I get bored in here once I die." He passed away in 1990 and true to his wishes, his gravestone stands as the closest one to the gate.

The Furnace and Mill

Some of the most important buildings that contributed to the profitability of the Hampton estate have unfortunately been lost to history. Most notable of these are the Northampton Iron Furnace and the Hampton Mill.

The Ridgely fortune was built on the production of iron. Northampton served as the primary furnace on the estate for almost seventy years. Begun in 1762 the Northampton Furnace first supplied quality pig iron to England and later to the Continental Army during the Revolutionary War. An advertisement in *The Maryland Gazette*, dated 1770, describes the furnace, casting house, bridge, and wheelhouse as being "built of stone." Operation of the forges ceased about 1850, and the Northampton Furnace

eventually fell into ruin before being covered by the completion of Loch Raven Reservoir in 1922.

In addition to the Northampton Furnace, Charles Carnan Ridgely acquired the Nottingham Furnace at White Marsh in 1812 and in 1820 he purchased the Curtis Creek Furnace property, formerly the Etna Ironworks on the Patapsco River in Anne Arundel County.

The ruins of the Iron Furnace revealed from under Loch Raven by a drought in 2002

The Hampton Mill, also known as the Ridgely Mill, directly supported the Northampton Furnace. Colonel Charles Ridgely's 1772 will refers to a gristmill seat containing a "pond and stream of water" and directs his heirs to "grind bread flour toll free for the Northampton Furnace. . . ." The Hampton Mill also supplied flour for the surrounding community as well as the Mansion. During the early 1780s the mill produced various grades of wheat flour such as "superfine," "seconds," "corn flour," and "ship stuff." In addition to flour, evidence shows that plaster, commonly used as fertilizer for the fields, was ground at the Mill.

The Hampton Mill, ca. 1895

The Ridgely Mill continued to be fairly profitable even after the closure of the Northampton Furnace by 1850. Refitted with new machinery in the 1860s, it was eventually rented out a decade later. Records reveal the expenses related to mill ownership including periodic storms that washed out the milldam, tenants that sometimes left the Ridgely Mill in "bad condition," and ongoing maintenance. In 1896 the old building was valued at only $300. It was abandoned some time in the early twentieth century, a victim to larger, more efficient mills in the Midwest.

11

The Gardens
and Grounds

A Chronological Overview

Hampton's gardens and grounds reflect nearly two hundred years of styles and trends in landscape architecture. Visitors can see the Falling Gardens of the late eighteenth century, the picturesque landscape principles of the early to mid-nineteenth century, and Colonial Revival design trends of the early twentieth century.

The Saucer Magnolia (Magnolia x soulangiana) in bloom in April

The social and cultural trends that shaped America and Hampton can be seen through the landscape. Formal gardens adorned the south side of the estate while fields of hay, corn, and other crops were planted on the north side. Extensive orchards once stretched to the east and west. The landscape with its original outbuildings form an unusually complete chronicle that reveals the daily activities of the Ridgely family, laborers, the enslaved, and tenant farmers from the eighteenth to the twentieth centuries.

The south façade of the Mansion with Great Terrace

Each generation of the Ridgelys expressed its personal tastes, which can still be seen at Hampton. The earliest designed landscape features were installed by Captain Charles Ridgely when the house was built. Found on the Great Terrace are two Catalpa trees dating to the time of the American Revolution. Earliest designs of the Parterres and boxwood plantings of Charles Carnan Ridgely reflect his influence on the property. Eliza Ridgely, third mistress of Hampton, was an avid horticulturalist. Her gardening legacy remains apparent not only with creation of the Victorian carpet bedding displayed in Parterre II, but in the plantings of many magnificent trees throughout the site, including the Cedar of Lebanon, the Paulownia, and the Saucer Magnolia.

Right: Carte de visite of Otho Ridgely standing by one of the garden urns, ca. 1862

Margaretta Sophia Ridgely and Helen West Stewart Ridgely, fourth and fifth

Marble urns were placed throughout the gardens at Hampton in the mid-nineteenth century

mistresses of Hampton, continued to plant thousands of colorful annuals and eventually modified the gardens to reduce the intense maintenance they required. The Parterre designs you see today reflect their influence during the late nineteenth century.

The historic front gates designed by John Laing in 1875

The Falling Gardens and Parterres

The jewel of Hampton's cultural landscape is the Falling Gardens. From the time the Falls were constructed in the late 1700s, this area of the property remained the focus of the family's horticultural pursuits for over 150 years. Just as the Mansion was situated to take advantage of sweeping views, the Falling Gardens were placed to take advantage of the natural topography of the hillside. Still, its construction has been described as one of the largest earthmoving projects of its time in America. Consisting of a series of flat terraces connected by grass slopes and ramps, Falling Gardens were a popular landscape feature of estates in the mid-Atlantic region. At Hampton, the dimensions of the terraces echo the dimensions of the main block of the Mansion, which together with rhythmic placement of marble urns fosters an architectural relationship between the house and garden.

American Scenery Architecture, &c.

Stereopticon view of Parterre I, 1872, by W. M. Chase

Planted on the terraces are a series of geometric gardens called Parterres (from the French "on the ground"). Originally developed during the medieval era as a method to avoid walking on cultivated soil, the style was later adapted for decorative use. The beauty of the plants is magnified by their close groupings and geometric patterns. The gardens, especially when seen from above, are astounding.

At Hampton, the Parterres were originally laid out by 1810 and are attributed to William Booth, a renowned designer of the period. The design of Parterre I dates from this early period. By mid-century, Eliza Ridgely—inspired by gardens she saw during her trips abroad—had introduced Victorian "carpet bedding," exotic varieties, and the fashionable marble urns. A published description of the parterres dating from 1875 testifies to the impressive sight: "The outlook over the Italian garden is most beautiful—rich in color, novel in effect. . . . In terrace after terrace, strictly kept distinct in masses of color, eight thousand plants are bedded out. The scarlet and orange and deep carmine of the geraniums; the blue and purple and white of the sweet-scented heliotropes; maroon and lavender of the verbenas; the tawney gold and red of the roses; and the ample leaves of the bronzy crimson and yellow of the coleus; the borderings of vivid green. . . ."

Pink peonies on lower Parterres

Restoration of the historic planting of Parterre I in 2009

The Orangery, the Greenhouses, and the Gardener's Cottage

Maintaining the ornate formal gardens, rare plants, and citrus fruits required a large labor force, talent, and specialized buildings. The core of the garden maintenance area consists of five buildings: the Caretaker's or Gardener's House, two Greenhouses, the Garden Maintenance Building for tool storage, and the Orangery.

Interior of one of the Greenhouses with plants, ca. 1940

The most elegant of these is Hampton's classically inspired Orangery, a reconstruction of the ca. 1830 Greek Revival structure. It was built to house citrus and other tender fruits that could not survive a Maryland winter out-of-doors. During the mid-nineteenth century, the Orangery at Hampton housed one of the finest citrus collections in the United States. The Ridgelys encircled the Great Terrace during the summer with over forty lemon and orange trees potted in tubs and paneled boxes. These plants were transferred to the Orangery for the winter. The Orangery was heated by solar energy through the full-length windows on the south and east

The mid-nineteenth century Greenhouses lie to the southwest of the Mansion and Orangery

The Orangery and west side of Mansion, 1908, by J. E. H. Post

sides, and by a hypocaust, a type of wood-burning furnace, in the west side shed. The hypocaust provided heat through flues that ran under the floor, radiating heat around the perimeter of the room and up the chimney.

The other buildings to support garden operations were located near the Falling Gardens. The Gardener's Cottage was built sometime before 1843 with later additions added around 1855. The first Greenhouse was built in the late 1830s, but was later Victorianized with decorative metalwork. The second Greenhouse was constructed in the early 1850s with a stone head house that contained the heating boiler, potting shed, and two small rooms for gardeners. The Garden Maintenance Building, an expansion of an ornamental cottage built around 1840, housed the horse-drawn mower and other gardening equipment. After rebuilding in the later part of the nineteenth century, it also contained housing for one or more of the garden staff.

The Entrance and the North Lawn

Descending from the Mansion to the cultivated fields of the Home Farm is the North Lawn, defined by masses of trees. Hampton Lane and the Carriage Drive leading to the Mansion frame the North Lawn. The historic entrance

The south façade of the Mansion in summer

drive retains much of its nineteenth-century character. Stately trees, a mix of evergreen and deciduous, line the road. Breaks in the tree line offer filtered views of the fields and Mansion. The North Lawn nearest the Mansion, encircled by the Heart-Shaped Drive, has few plantings today but once featured many trees and beds of roses.

The Stable Lane to the east, an important link between the Mansion and Home Farm, offers a less elegant counterpoint to the Carriage Drive. Designed more for service, it provides access to the Stables and domestic service buildings near the Mansion. A second branch of this lane winds down to the Family Cemetery.

The open landscape of the North Lawn is a wonderful specimen of the English Landscape style, which was pioneered in the United States by renowned landscape architects, including Andrew Jackson Downing. This landscape design featuring mature specimen trees in informal groupings looks natural, but is in reality carefully contrived. From the Mansion, the view of the Home Farm represents a little village amid a pastoral landscape. From the Home Farm, the imposing Mansion rests astride the hilltop, framed by large trees like the border of a painting.

The north façade of the Mansion in the fall (photo: Richard Anderson)

12

Period Rooms
in the Mansion

Investigating the Past:
The Curator as Detective

A great deal of detective work is needed to accurately recreate the historic interiors at Hampton. Fortunately, the extensive collection of objects with Ridgely family provenance and related archival collections, including literally millions of documents and thousands of historic photographs, are the basis for the exhaustive research that underlies all the room reinstallation efforts. In Hampton's Music Room (1870–1890), for example, a photograph from the 1880s showed one of the windows in summertime, with just lace curtains and a painted window shade in use. Hampton's curators were able to match the distinctive motifs seen in the

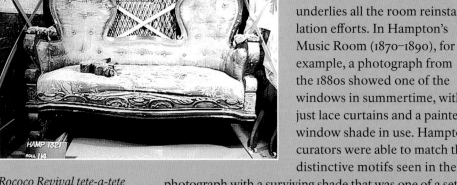

*Rococo Revival tete-a-tete
from the Drawing Room,
before conservation*

photograph with a surviving shade that was one of a set of three featuring allegories of Music, Theater, and Gardening. Hand-painted reproductions were commissioned which meticulously recreate even the style of the brush

Rococo Revival tete-a-tete from the Drawing Room, after conservation and reupholstery

The southwest window in Music Room with reproduction of the original shade

strokes. Also for the Music Room, staff discovered a set of three yellow-gold silk damask lambrequin valances with Hampton provenance in the collection of the Maryland Historical Society. The three valances measurements and hardware precisely match the gilt window cornices made for the Music Room in 1851. Here too, reproductions were fabricated using documented fabric and trimmings.

This same silk damask was also used in Hampton's Drawing Room during the mid-nineteenth century, but in a brilliant shade of crimson rather than yellow. Around 1845, Eliza Ridgely purchased a suite of Rococo Revival seating furniture for the Drawing Room. Examinations showed the tete-a-tete had never been reupholstered and that fragments of the first top cover were present. An unfaded piece of the fabric, large enough to both confirm the pattern and for use in dye-matching the reproduction damask, was found in the space between the seat and the back. Another tiny surviving swatch of fabric confirmed that the window curtains were also made of the same material. Further evidence for curtain treatments for the Drawing Room was located in a trunk containing numerous pieces of curtains and trimmings originally used in the Mansion. These included a very large (eleven inches) and elaborate single tassel in crimson and cream silk, a matching double tassel curtain tie-back, and original 1840s embroidered sheer muslin curtains which feature "tambour" or chain stitch in an intricate pattern. Custom-made reproductions of all these materials were created for the Drawing Room.

The recreation of the Drawing Room wallpaper was even more complex. Several historic photos of the room, dating from 1885 to 1910, show floral wallpaper with a foliate border. Leading wallpaper experts dated it to the late 1830s. Modern computer technology allowed the enlargement of images of the pattern to its actual size. Colors were determined from the palette of other antique French wallpapers, studying botanical prints of the period, and the natural colors of the elements. The resulting reproduction wallpaper and border makes a bold statement of the taste of the times.

Helen Ridgely in front of the pier mirror in Drawing Room showing adjacent wallpaper, ca. 1895

While fewer original materials survive from the earlier eras, documentary evidence can supply the information necessary to authentically recreate a period room setting. In Hampton's colorful Dining Room (1810–1929), for example, the window treatments are documented by a citation in Governor Ridgely's 1829 estate inventory: "3 blue silk window curtains, yellow and blue drapery."

This reflects the paint colors original to the 1810s (Prussian blue and yellow ochre). Further, the original gilded cornices used in the room date from this time and are the type specifically fashioned to use with drapery valances. The specific design used for the reproduction curtains is based on a plate in a book by Pierre de la Mesangère (Paris, ca. 1815) owned by the Ridgelys.

Left: The Drawing Room pier mirror and reproduction of the nineteenth-century wallpaper

The Parlour

The Parlour at Hampton is furnished to the earliest period of Ridgely family occupancy (1790–1810). With its early date and less formal style, the Parlour provides visual and

The north wall of the Parlour

cultural contrast to the later, more ornate rooms. During the Federal era, the Parlour would have functioned much as a sitting or family room does today. More typical of mid-eighteenth-century usage, however, the room was also used as a bed-chamber during the period of eighteen months that Captain Charles Ridgely (1733–1790) "The Builder" resided in the Mansion. He died in his bed in this room in June 1790, after suffering a stroke in his office in the west hyphen. The Parlour now primarily reflects the tastes and lifestyle of the Captain's nephew and principal heir, Governor Charles Carnan Ridgely (1760–1829), and his wife Priscilla Hill Dorsey (1762–1814). As Mrs. Ridgely was an ardent Methodist, however, the ostentation and lavish furnishings seen in later rooms at Hampton are not present here. The room is now usually arranged to show informal activities such as a lady's morning room or family tea party.

Federal armchair made by John Shaw for the Maryland Senate, 1797

Many records such as bills and receipts survive that document numerous purchases of house furnishing materials for Hampton in the early 1790s. These have been used to guide the selections of materials for the room, including "moreen" upholstery and curtain fabric, a woven wool with an embossed watered pattern. Similarly, the use of an English Wilton carpet with an oriental type pattern dating from around 1800 reflects Governor Ridgely's order for two Turkey carpets through import merchant Andrew Buchanan in 1793. The wallpaper with a design

referred to in the period as an "arabesque" is a reproduction of an American paper inspired by French neoclassical designs. The room is also filled with noteworthy objects original to the Federal period, including Hampton's earliest set of chairs, possibly the work of Baltimore cabinetmaker William Askew (fl. 1780–1786), who is documented as having made furniture for the Ridgelys at this early period. The portraits of "The Builder" and his wife by John Hesselius also reside here, as they have since at least the 1850s.

The Parlour's Federal era furnishings include a set of chairs made for the Ridgelys in the 1780s.

Chinese export porcelain punch bowl, ca. 1810

The Dining Room

The Dining Room is furnished to represent Hampton between 1810 and 1829 when Governor Charles Carnan Ridgely died. The settings seen in the Dining Room exemplify what was expected of people of the social rank of the Ridgelys and reflect the Governor's sophisticated taste and wealth. The man known to "keep the best table in America" even employed a French cook who traveled back and forth between Annapolis, Baltimore, and Hampton. The room also reflects the preparation and service by Governor Ridgely's slaves, at least twelve of whom worked in the Mansion.

Baltimore Empire cellarette, used to store wine bottles, ca. 1820

Looking toward the east at Yuletide, with the table set for a formal dinner

By the time of Hampton's construction, separate rooms for eating had become common in large houses. Dinner was served in the mid-to-late afternoon and might consist of several courses. Seasonally, the Hampton table setting is changed, representing the first course of a sumptuous dinner in winter, with two tablecloths and all the plates and service dishes in an orderly, symmetrical pattern. An elegant dessert course is displayed in summer, with cloths removed and an elaborate silver epergne with fruits and sweetmeats displayed in the center of the table. The sideboard features an ostentatious display of family silver at all times.

The Dining Room paint colors (Prussian blue and ocher), based upon scientific analysis, replicate the second layer of paint, ca. 1810. The scenic wallpaper, "Monuments of Paris," reproduces a fashionable French paper available at shops close by the Governor's townhouse in Baltimore.

The Dining Room in summer, with the table set for the dessert course

The window treatments reflect a citation in Governor Ridgely's 1829 estate inventory: "3 blue silk window curtains, yellow and blue drapery," and are based on a plate by Pierre de la Mesangère (Paris, ca. 1815) owned by the Ridgelys.

Around 1810, the door in the northeast corner of the Dining Room was added to give direct access to an expanded butler's pantry and the kitchen beyond. Governor Ridgely also purchased a number of pieces of furniture specifically for the room beginning about the time of this renovation. Most were made in Baltimore in the 1810–1825 period and are stylish examples of the Late Neoclassical or Empire taste.

Baltimore Empire secretary attributed to William Camp, ca. 1820

The Drawing Room

The Drawing Room was Hampton Mansion's most formal room, at all periods filled with the best furniture and decorations. It was primarily used to receive guests, entertain visitors, for after-dinner receptions, and other special occasions. Conversations by mid-nineteenth century guests as they enjoyed the Ridgelys' hospitality might have reflected international events, some of which (such as the European Revolutions of 1848) the family directly encountered during their travels. Even more likely, the discussions may have been dominated by events of more national and local concern, reflecting the sectional strife then rampant, especially within a border state like Maryland.

The southeast corner of the Drawing Room

Baltimore Empire painted sofa (detail, swan arm) by John Finlay, 1832

The room is furnished to represent the period of 1830–1860 when John and Eliza Ridgely were master and mistress of Hampton. The setting especially reflects Eliza, a woman of great taste and sophistication. Eliza and John also traveled widely, taking four extended tours of Europe in the 1830s to 1850s. An observer once described the Drawing Room at Hampton as "richly adorned with statuary and objects of vertu gathered in foreign lands." Souvenirs collected during the Ridgelys' trips abroad can be seen in the room.

Surviving bills, accounts, and travel records document Eliza's purchases of the most fashionable objects to furnish Hampton, in the United States as well as Europe. The

The Drawing Room furnishings reflect mid-nineteenth-century taste

room combines elements of both the Neoclassical and Romantic Revival styles from the second quarter of the nineteenth century. Of primary importance is the suite of Neoclassical painted furniture purchased in 1832 from John Finlay, the most important maker of Baltimore painted furniture. A second Rococo Revival parlor set made in Baltimore around 1845 was based on designs by Thomas King. A pair of enormous, custom-made gilded pier mirrors and matching window cornices bearing the family coat of arms were supplied to the Ridgelys around 1843. The crimson silk damask upholstery and curtain fabric, curtain trimmings, tambour embroidered sheer curtains, and Rococo-style English carpet are all reproductions of surviving Ridgely family originals in the Hampton NHS collection. The floral wallpaper with foliate border was recreated from a paper dating ca. 1840 seen in late-nineteenth-century photos of the room.

Portrait of Charles Carnan Ridgely, Jr., by J. W. Jarvis, ca. 1812

The Music Room

Harp made for Eliza Ridgely by Sebastian Erard of London, 1817

The southwest parlor at Hampton has been known as the Music Room since at least the 1840s, though it served other purposes including that of the principal library in the house. Musical instruments, including the piano and the harp, were always present and often used to entertain guests. As one visitor to Hampton recorded in the 1840s, "We had some music after dinner—she [Eliza Ridgely (1803–1867), Hampton's third mistress] singing some Italian songs for me & I playing some of my best pieces for her. Her harp stood there uncovered. . . ." That harp, purchased for Eliza by her father, Nicholas Greenbury Ridgely, from Erard of London in 1817, still stands in the Music Room today. As furnished now, the room accurately reflects the taste of the high Victorian era, 1870–1890. Margaretta Howard Ridgely (1824–1904), widow of Hampton's fourth master Charles Ridgely (1830–1872), was then mistress of the household. Though only infrequently making major purchases of furnishings, she did acquire an important musical instrument, the Steinway square grand piano made in New York in 1878.

The Music Room looking south in winter (photo: Richard Anderson)

The Music Room dressed for summer

Probate inventories and historic photographs, some dating as early as the mid-1880s, show the Music Room filled with furnishings from previous periods and the walls densely hung with paintings. These include portraits of family members ranging from the early nineteenth century to the late 1870s plus a variety of other works such as landscapes and old master paintings the Ridgelys collected on their numerous trips abroad. The exceptionally large and ornate gilded pier mirror and matching window cornices featuring the Ridgely family stag's head crest were made for the room by Samson Cariss of Baltimore in May 1851. The yellow silk damask lambrequin window valances copy the originals in the collection of the Maryland Historical Society. Hand-painted window shades, exact copies of the originals in Hampton's collection, feature allegories of Music, Theater, and Gardening. Other distinctive Ridgely family pieces in the room, all of Baltimore manufacture, include a very large three-part Rococo Revival sofa (ca. 1850) and a lady's slipper chair made for Eliza Ridgely by the city's leading cabinetmaker, Robert Renwick, in 1858.

Ladies playing piano in the Music Room, ca. 1895

The Great Hall

The Great Hall at the center of the main block of Hampton Mansion is an extraordinary space measuring fifty-one feet by twenty-one feet. Sometimes referred to as the soul of the house, it has served many diverse purposes over the years. Devout Methodist and first mistress Rebecca Dorsey Ridgely (1740–1812) "inaugurated her housewarming by religious services and a watch meeting in the large-hall." More convivial events were held there during Governor Charles Carnan Ridgely's (1760–1829) time, including large parties and balls, one guest recording "Fifty-one People sat down to Dinner in the Hall and had plenty of room." Eliza Eichelberger Ridgely (1803–1867) acquired many of the fine furnishings, art, and decorations for the space, including several pairs of magnificent Chinese porcelain palace jars, the largest of which are still placed along the east wall. Despite such impressive

Stained-glass fanlight in the Great Hall, 1845, and carved plaque with Ridgely coat of arms

The Great Hall looking south

Italian landscape painting attributed to Leonardo Coccorante and Giovanni Marziale, 1740

and fragile decorations, Eliza's children Charles and Didy exercised, rolled hoops, and threw snowballs in the Great Hall. Some years later, the room was the site of Didy's wedding to John Campbell White. There were also more somber occasions, including the funerals of both Eliza and her husband John Ridgely (1790–1867) and some family servants. In the twentieth century the room was again the site of large gatherings, including debutant balls and other festivities.

In the mid-nineteenth century, the installation of stained glass in the four principal windows and lights over the doors gave the room a chapel-like appearance. It was then filled with furniture of several periods. Leopard skins, first ordered from Paris by Eliza Ridgely in the 1830s, covered the floor. On the walls were massed numerous family portraits, including Thomas Sully's famous 1818 depiction of the beautiful young Eliza Ridgely, *Lady with a Harp*. Many other pictures, including very large eighteenth-century Italian landscapes, were purchased by the Ridgelys during their grand tours of Europe. Although somewhat more sparsely furnished today, the Great Hall is a space that introduces the visitor to the history of Hampton, generations of the Ridgely family, and the story of the estate's preservation.

Baltimore Federal painted armchair from the set owned by John Eager Howard, ca. 1810

89

The Master Bedchamber with embroidered summer bed and window hangings

The Master Bedchamber

Baltimore Federal night table (commode), ca. 1800 (photo: Lanny Layman)

This southwest room on the second floor was historically used as the principal bedchamber at Hampton. It is furnished to represent the occupancy of the second master and mistress, Governor Charles Carnan Ridgely (1760–1829) and his wife, Priscilla Hill Dorsey (1762–1814). During this period, guests might be received in the bedchamber, thus the elaborate nature of the room's decoration and furnishings. The ornate architectural features are painted to replicate the original polychrome marbleized chimneypiece and Prussian blue woodwork with ocher dentils. The landscape painting over the mantel was copied from a late-eighteenth-century view of Baltimore by George Beck now at the Maryland Historical Society. The wallpaper reproduces a "floral trail" pattern of the 1790s, based on a citation for "flowered paper" in Governor Ridgely's estate inventory. Also of floral design is the reproduction wool Brussels-type carpet (loop-pile woven in twenty-seven-inch strips), copied in England from a pattern dated 1793.

Priscilla bore at least fourteen children between 1783 and 1803. During a woman's "lying-in" after the birth of a child, friends and neighbors would have visited, making the room semipublic and necessitating plenty of chairs, such as the large set of Maryland-made chairs probably in use at Hampton since around 1790. Beds with their accompanying textiles were among the most important and valuable objects in the house. The large Baltimore mahogany bed, circa 1800, was sold by the Ridgelys in the 1930s but brought back to Hampton in 2002 after it was purchased at auction by Historic Hampton, Inc. The bed hangings exhibited in the winter are a reproduction of a polychrome floral chintz from the 1790s, reflecting Priscilla Ridgley's purchases of furnishing textiles in that period. The summer seasonal change shows bed hangings and matching window curtains of sheer white muslin with tambour embroidery in blue, based on an original Hampton bed valance in the collection of the Maryland Historical Society. The room furnishings feature both a lady's muslin-draped dressing table with accoutrements and a gentleman's elaborate English dressing table (sometimes called a "Beau Brummel"), veneered with West Indian satinwood.

"Beau Brummel" English Hepplewhite gentleman's dressing table, ca. 1800

The west wall of the Master Bedchamber in winter (photo: Lanny Layman)

The Northeast Bedchamber

This second-floor room has been selected to interpret the daily life of the children of Hampton in the mid-nineteenth century when John Ridgely (1790–1867) and his wife Eliza Eichelberger Ridgely (1803–1867) were master and mistress of Hampton. Their two surviving children, Eliza called "Didy" (1828–1894) and Charles (1830–1872) grew up at Hampton, and their bedrooms were on this floor. Later, after Charles married his first cousin Margaretta Howard in 1851, they also raised a family of eight children at Hampton. Didy and Charles were educated both at home by tutors (who resided on the Mansion's third floor) and at boarding schools in town in Baltimore. Both children frequently brought their school friends home to spend the weekends with them in the country, where they enjoyed a wide range of both indoor and outdoor activities. Objects in the room reflect both the lighter side of childhood (dolls and toys) and the more serious side (school books, an invalid feeder). There are also references to even more

The Northeast Bedchamber at Yuletide

special events, such as books and souvenirs from the trips to Europe that Ridgely family children enjoyed in this period.

Watercolor of a children's dancing party in Baltimore, ca. 1843

The room setting accurately reflects the mid-nineteenth-century period at Hampton, including the fashionable mint green paint on the woodwork and the reproduction wallpaper, copied from a Rococo Revival style pattern used in an English country house around 1850. The large Turkey carpet may be one of the "Smyrna" carpets ordered for Hampton in the 1850s. The mahogany furniture in the Late Neoclassical taste dates from 1820 to 1840 and is original to the house. The pair of wardrobes are reminders that even a house as grand as Hampton had no built-in closets in its bedchambers. The maple tall post bed was made around 1830, probably in the shop of John Needles, Baltimore's leading Quaker cabinetmaker and known abolitionist. Its narrow size suggests its use as a youth bed. Bed covers of purple ground floral chintz quilt in winter and embroidered white work bedspread in summer are from the site's extensive collection of Ridgely owned furnishing textiles.

Doll's Paris porcelain dinner service and Baltimore repoussé silver tea set by S. Kirk, ca. 1840

The Guest Bedchamber

The Guest (northwest) Bedchamber is furnished to the 1890–1910 period, a time at Hampton when the Ridgely family fortunes had begun to wane. For much of the nineteenth and into the twentieth century, the room was called the "White Curtain Room" because white muslin window and bed curtains with distinctive red and white trimming were in use from about 1835 to 1948. The woodwork was similarly painted white for much of this time period. Bringing the exhibits at Hampton into the twentieth century, the room also highlights the era and accomplishments of Helen Stewart Ridgely (1852–1927), wife of Captain John Ridgely (1851–1937). A focal point of the room is the pastel portrait of Helen over the mantelpiece, done in 1904 by noted Baltimore artist Florence Mackubin. Helen was a highly accomplished woman, noted as the author of two books in addition to numerous civic activities and an active role in managing the estate. The installation suggests that a female friend has come to visit Helen and will be staying in the guest room, thus the display of suitcase, small trunk, hatbox, and other travel-related items.

Paris porcelain veilleuse (teapot on warming stand), ca. 1830

The Guest Bedchamber looking toward the northwest (photo: Lanny Layman)

Top of a Federal bureau with ladies' dressing accessories (photo: Lanny Layman)

In the winter seasonal display, a lady's riding habit, hat, and boots suggest the visitor will go fox-hunting with the Ridgelys, a favorite family pastime.

The furnishings reflect the typical patterns of turn-of-the-century Baltimore, when an accumulation of objects from several periods and styles would have been in use. Furniture ranges in date from the earliest period of Ridgely ownership (a Chippendale blanket chest, ca. 1785) up to more recent pieces (chairs from a large Renaissance Revival bedroom suite given to Captain John and Helen Ridgely at the time of their marriage in 1873 by his mother, Margaretta Howard Ridgely). The dressing table and bureau have been furnished with all the accoutrements necessary for a lady's comfort and convenience, including a silver dresser set, perfume bottles, cosmetic jars, jewelry cases, glove stretcher, and numerous other items, almost all owned originally by the Ridgelys. The room-sized Turkey carpet was purchased for Hampton by John and Eliza Ridgely in the late 1850s.

English corner washstand, ca. 1810, with English ironstone china washstand set by J. & W. Ridgway, ca. 1830 (photo: Lanny Layman)

Acknowledgments

The National Park Service at Hampton National Historic Site would like to acknowledge the following individuals who were responsible for the content contained in this guidebook: Gay Vietzke, Superintendent; Vince Vaise, Chief of Interpretation; Paul Bitzel, Chief of Resource Management; Gregory Weidman, Curator; Debbie Patterson, Registrar; Kirby Shedlowski, Park Ranger; Paul Plamann, Park Ranger; Catherine Holden, Seasonal Park Ranger; and Julia Lehnert, Archivist.

Modern images found in the guidebook were contributed by the following people: Debbie Patterson, Bill Curtis, Barbara Vietzke, Tim Ervin, Lanny Layman, Richard Anderson, and Carol Highsmith. Artwork was done by Richard Schlecht.

Historic Hampton, Inc., the primary non-profit partner and friends group for Hampton NHS, graciously supported the production of this book. Special thanks to Robert Brown, President, and the entire Board for their support.